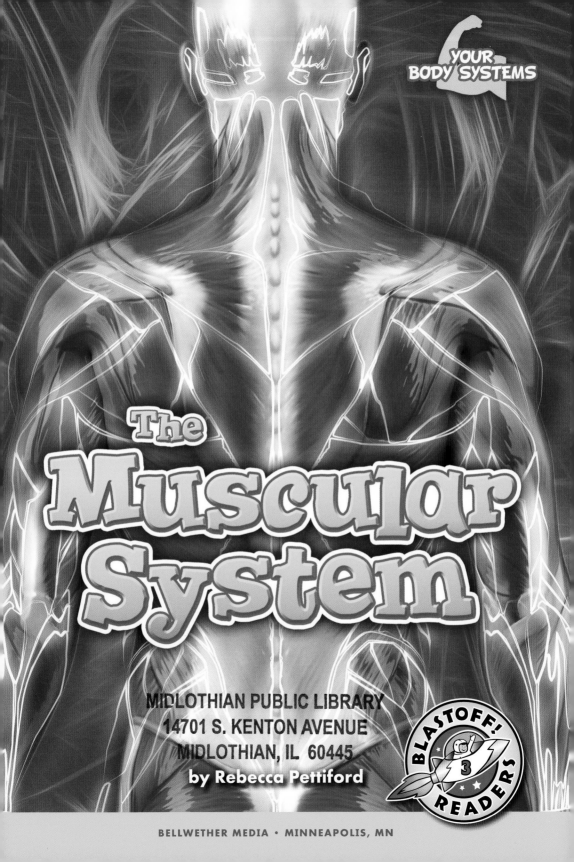

YOUR BODY SYSTEMS

The Muscular System

by Rebecca Pettiford

BLASTOFF! READERS
3

BELLWETHER MEDIA · MINNEAPOLIS, MN

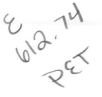

E
612.74
PET

Note to Librarians, Teachers, and Parents:

Blastoff! Readers are carefully developed by literacy experts and combine standards-based content with developmentally appropriate text.

Level 1 provides the most support through repetition of high-frequency words, light text, predictable sentence patterns, and strong visual support.

Level 2 offers early readers a bit more challenge through varied simple sentences, increased text load, and less repetition of high-frequency words.

Level 3 advances early-fluent readers toward fluency through increased text and concept load, less reliance on visuals, longer sentences, and more literary language.

Level 4 builds reading stamina by providing more text per page, increased use of punctuation, greater variation in sentence patterns, and increasingly challenging vocabulary.

Level 5 encourages children to move from "learning to read" to "reading to learn" by providing even more text, varied writing styles, and less familiar topics.

Whichever book is right for your reader, Blastoff! Readers are the perfect books to build confidence and encourage a love of reading that will last a lifetime!

This edition first published in 2020 by Bellwether Media, Inc.

No part of this publication may be reproduced in whole or in part without written permission of the publisher. For information regarding permission, write to Bellwether Media, Inc., Attention: Permissions Department, 6012 Blue Circle Drive, Minnetonka, MN 55343.

Library of Congress Cataloging-in-Publication Data

Names: Pettiford, Rebecca, author.
Title: The Muscular System / by Rebecca Pettiford.
Description: Minneapolis, MN : Bellwether Media, Inc., 2020. | Series: Blastoff! Readers: Your Body Systems | Audience: Age 5-8. | Audience: K to grade 3. | Includes bibliographical references and index.
Identifiers: LCCN 2018056084 (print) | LCCN 2018057529 (ebook) | ISBN 9781618915610 (ebook) | ISBN 9781644870204 (hardcover : alk. paper) | ISBN 9781618917539 (pbk. : alk. paper)
Subjects: LCSH: Muscles–Juvenile literature. | Muscular system–Juvenile literature.
Classification: LCC QM151 (ebook) | LCC QM151 .P49 2020 (print) | DDC 612.7/4–dc23
LC record available at https://lccn.loc.gov/2018056084

Editor: Rebecca Sabelko   Designer: Brittany McIntosh

Printed in the United States of America, North Mankato, MN.

Table of Contents

What Is the Muscular System?

There are over 600 muscles in the human body! They make up the muscular system. They create movement in the body.

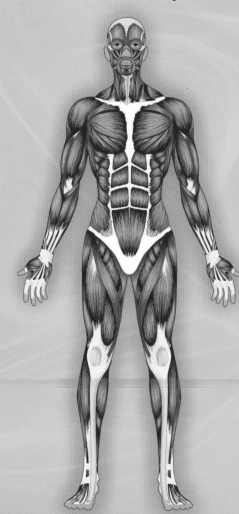

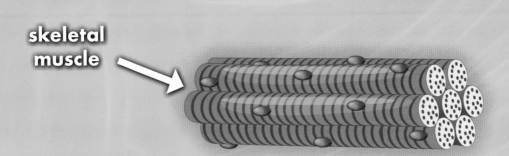

skeletal
muscle

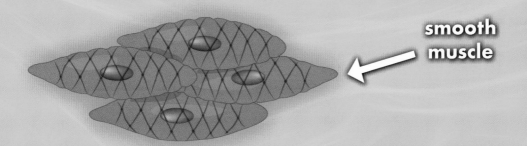

smooth
muscle

cardiac
muscle

The human body has **skeletal**,
smooth, and **cardiac** muscles.
Each type has a special purpose!

Cardiac muscles push blood through the **circulatory system**.

blood cells

Smooth muscles move **nutrients** through the body. Skeletal muscles let us move around.

How Does the Muscular System Work?

All muscles shorten and lengthen. This creates movement. The brain sends signals to the muscles through the **nervous system**. The signals tell the muscles to **contract**.

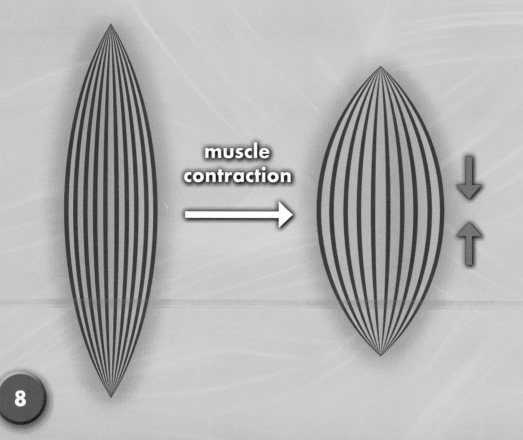

muscle contraction

skeletal muscle

Skeletal muscles are **voluntary**. We decide when to move them.

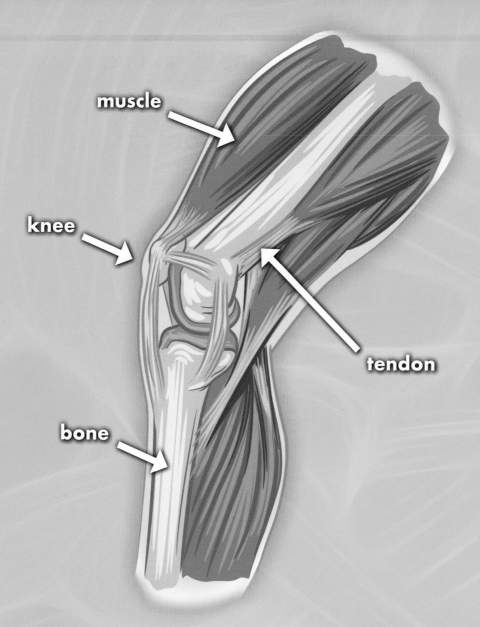

muscle

knee

tendon

bone

Tendons connect skeletal muscles to bones. These muscles come in pairs.

For example, the **bicep** muscle pulls on the tendon when it contracts. The arm bends. The **tricep** muscle lengthens.

bicep

tricep

bicep muscle
contracting

bicep
pulls tendon

There are two types of skeletal muscles. **Slow-twitch muscles** can work for a long time. They are good for distance running and biking.

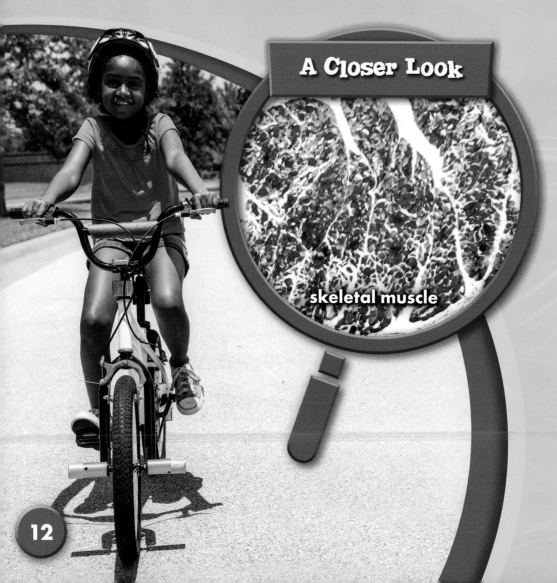

A Closer Look

skeletal muscle

Fast-twitch muscles are
good for quick blasts of speed
or strength.

heart

cardiac
muscle

Cardiac muscles move
blood through the body.

The heart is an **involuntary** muscle. The nervous system tells the heart how slow or fast to pump.

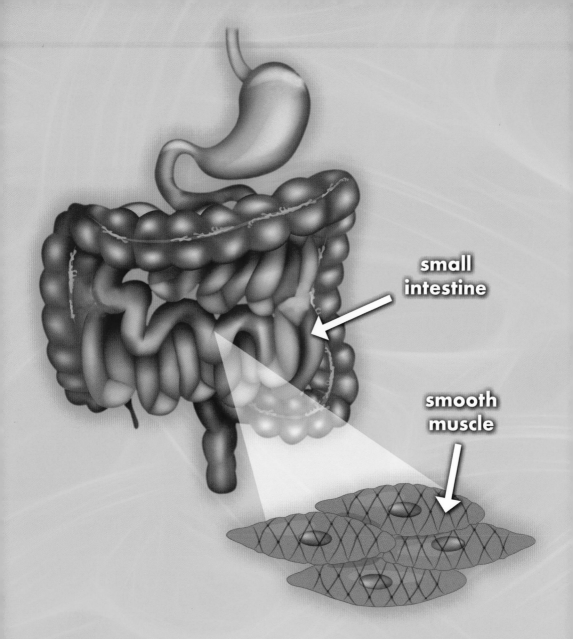

small intestine

smooth muscle

Smooth muscles are also involuntary. They are in the walls of some **organs**.

Smooth muscles work like waves.
They are found in the stomach.
The muscles in the stomach walls
move food.

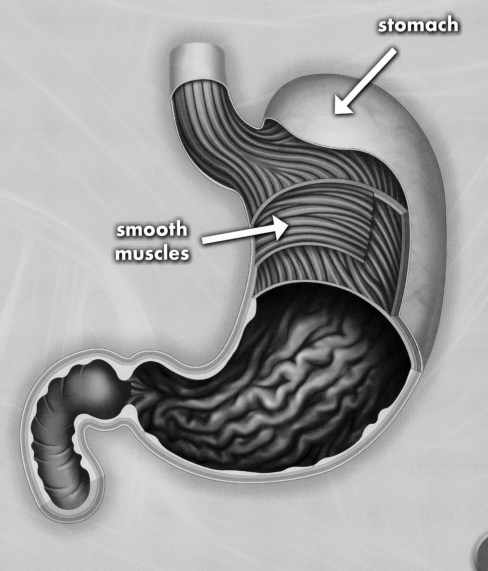

stomach

smooth
muscles

Why Is the Muscular System Important?

We could not walk or play sports without muscles. We could not eat or breathe. The heart could not beat.

We could not live without
a muscular system!

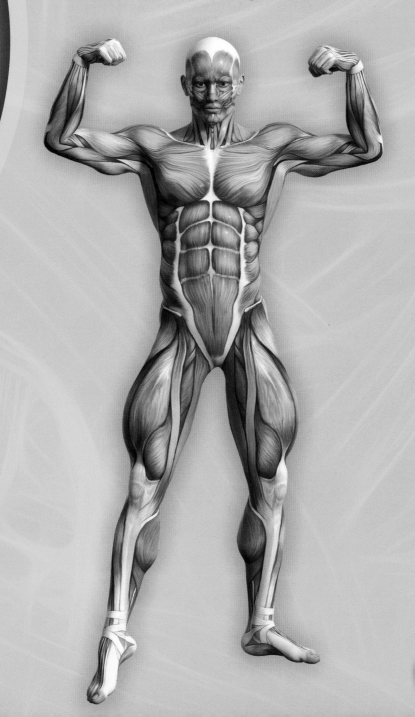

It is important to take care of our muscles. Eating well helps them grow. Sleep helps repair them. Muscles can shrink and become weak if we do not use them. Exercise makes them strong!

Your Cardiac Muscle at Work!

Your cardiac muscle is powerful!

You will need:
- two large buckets that are the same size
- 16 cups of water
- 1/4 measuring cup
- a timer

1. Fill one bucket with 16 cups of water.

2. Place this bucket next to the empty bucket.

3. Set a timer for 1 minute. Using the 1/4 measuring cup, move all the water in the bucket into the empty bucket in 1 minute or less.

Could you do it? It takes your heart about 72 beats to move this amount of blood through your body in one minute!

Glossary

bicep—the large muscle at the front of the upper arm

cardiac—relating to the heart

circulatory system—the organs that move blood through the body

contract—to shorten

fast-twitch muscles—muscles that shorten quickly

involuntary—something that is done without choice

nervous system—the system that sends messages for controlling movement between the brain and other parts of the body

nutrients—the things humans need to live and grow

organs—parts of the body that have a particular job

skeletal—relating to the skeleton or bones of the body

slow-twitch muscles—muscles that shorten slowly

tendons—cords of tissue that connect muscle to bone

tricep—the large muscle along the back of the upper arm

voluntary—something that is done by choice

To Learn More

AT THE LIBRARY
Brett, Flora. *Your Muscular System Works!* North Mankato, Minn.: Capstone Press, 2015.

Cole, Tayler. *20 Fun Facts About the Muscular System.* New York, N.Y.: Gareth Stevens Publishing, 2019.

Kenney, Karen Latchana. *Muscular System.* Minneapolis, Minn.: Jump!, 2017.

ON THE WEB

Factsurfer.com gives you a safe, fun way to find more information.

1. Go to www.factsurfer.com.

2. Enter "muscular system" into the search box and click 🔍.

3. Select your book cover to see a list of related web sites.

Index